TRADITIONAL CHINESE MEDICINE AND EMOTIONAL BALANCE

FOR NOVICES

Balancing Mind And Body Through Time-Honored Practices - A Journey To Emotional Well-Being With TCM Insights

DR. TADEO KASEN

Table of Contents

2

DISCLIAMER

This book is intended for informational and educational purposes only. The content provided in this book is not a substitute for professional medical advice, diagnosis, or treatment. Always seek the advice of your physician or other qualified health provider with any questions you may have regarding a medical condition.

The techniques and practices described in this book are based on general principles and may not be suitable for everyone. Individual results may vary, and it is important to consult with a qualified healthcare professional before undertaking any new health or wellness program.

The author and publisher of this book are not responsible for any adverse effects or consequences resulting from the use of information, suggestions, exercises, or techniques presented herein. The reader assumes full responsibility for his or her actions and choices. The information provided in this book is accurate and reliable. However, the author and publisher make no representation or warranties of any kind, express or implied, regarding the completeness, accuracy, reliability, or suitability of the information provided.

Any References to specific products, services, or organizations do not imply endorsement or recommendation by the author.

By reading this book, the reader acknowledges and agrees to the terms of this disclaimer. If the reader does not agree with these terms, they should not use the information provided in this book.

CHAPTER ONE

Traditional Chinese Medicine Overview

Traditional Chinese Medicine (TCM) is a holistic healthcare approach that has been practiced for thousands of years in China and other East Asian countries. It refers to a variety of traditional therapeutic approaches that have evolved throughout time to address a wide range of health issues. Unlike Western medicine, which focuses on specific symptoms or diseases, TCM takes a more holistic approach, trying to restore balance and harmony to the entire body.

TCM is based on the notion that the body is a complex system of interrelated components, and that health is maintained when these parts are in harmony. This holistic viewpoint takes into account not just the physical body but also the mind and soul. TCM practitioners frequently highlight the significance of emotional and mental well-being as essential components of total health.

Traditional Chinese Medicine Fundamentals

TCM is based on a set of fundamental principles that govern its diagnostic and therapeutic procedures. Qi (pronounced "chee") is a basic notion that is sometimes interpreted as vital energy or life force. Qi runs through the body via precise paths known as meridians, according to TCM. Qi balance and free flow are critical for optimum health, but blockages or imbalances can lead to sickness.

The idea of Yin and Yang is another fundamental principle. Yin and Yang are opposing but complementary natural energies that are used to describe the dualism nature of different phenomena, including the human body.

The dynamic balance of these two forces is considered as health, and TCM therapies frequently try to restore equilibrium when there is an excess or deficit of Yin or Yang.

Traditional Chinese Medicine's Yin And Yang

Yin and Yang are key ideas in Traditional Chinese Medicine philosophy, signifying the dynamic balance of opposing forces in the cosmos and inside the human body. Stillness, darkness, cold, and substance are connected with Yin, while activity, light, heat, and function are associated with Yang. Organs and physiological processes in the human body are classified as either Yin or Yang.

For optimal health, Yin and Yang must be in harmony. An imbalance in which one force outweighs the other might result in a variety of health problems.

An excess of Yang, for example, can cause symptoms such as restlessness, sleeplessness, and hypertension, whereas an excess of Yin can cause lethargy, chilly extremities, and edema. TCM therapies frequently try to balance Yin and Yang to restore equilibrium and enhance general well-being.

The Theory Of The Five Elements

Another fundamental component of TCM is the Five Elements Theory, which provides a framework for understanding the links between various parts of the body and the natural environment.

Wood, Fire, Earth, Metal, and Water are connected with distinct organs, seasons, emotions, and other characteristics. These components' interactions are thought to impact health and illness.

Each element is connected with a pair of organs and a set of feelings. The Wood element, for example, is related to the liver and gallbladder and is associated with feelings of rage and fury.

Understanding these linkages enables TCM practitioners to recognize patterns of discord and adapt therapies to address both the physical and emotional components of a person's well-being.

Qi (Chi) Is A Term Used In Traditional Chinese Medicine.

Qi is a key concept in Traditional Chinese Medicine, signifying the vital energy that circulates through the body and maintains life. It is the animating power of the body and is in charge of all physiological activities. Illness develops when the flow of Qi is disrupted or imbalanced, according to TCM theory.

Acupuncture, herbal medicine, and Qigong are among the practices used to restore the correct flow of Qi and promote healing. Acupuncture, for example, entails inserting small needles into particular places throughout the body's meridians to unblock Qi and restore equilibrium. Herbal therapy makes use of herbs and minerals to regulate Qi and treat particular imbalances.

Traditional Chinese Medicine's Meridian System

The Meridian System is a network of Qi-flowing canals or routes. These meridians connect the organs and tissues of the body, offering a detailed picture of important energy flow. There are twelve major meridians, each associated with a different organ and related to different physiological and emotional activities.

TCM practitioners use the Meridian System to aid diagnosis and therapy. They can discover imbalances and customize remedies to restore harmony by analyzing the quality and flow of Qi in different meridians. Acupuncture, acupressure, and other treatments frequently target particular spots along these meridians to regulate Qi flow and manage a variety of health conditions.

Finally, Traditional Chinese Medicine provides a comprehensive and time-tested approach to health that takes into account the interdependence of the body, mind, and spirit. Fundamental TCM ideas such as Yin and Yang, the Five Elements Theory, Qi, and the Meridian System give a framework for understanding health and illness.

TCM seeks to restore balance and enhance the body's intrinsic ability to heal itself by treating both the physical and emotional components of well-being. This holistic approach to healthcare continues to connect with those looking for alternatives to Western medicine, emphasizing the significance of emotional balance in overall health.

CHAPTER TWO

Traditional Chinese Medicine Diagnosis

Traditional Chinese medicine (TCM) takes a different approach to diagnosis than Western medicine. The emphasis in TCM is on understanding the body's balance and harmony. Diagnosis entails an in-depth examination of different elements, such as the patient's symptoms, medical history, and observation of subtle signals. TCM practitioners use a holistic approach, taking into account the interconnection of the body, mind, and spirit.

The balance of Qi, the essential life energy that runs through the body's meridians, is a crucial notion in TCM diagnosis. The meridians are energy channels that connect various organs and systems. Illnesses are said to be caused by imbalances or obstructions in the flow of Qi. TCM practitioners examine Qi and general health using four basic diagnostic methods: observation, hearing and smelling, questioning, and palpation.

Examining the patient's appearance, particularly the complexion, tongue, and body motions, is part of the observation process. The tongue is very important in TCM diagnosis since its color, coating, and shape reveal information about the status of internal organs. A pale tongue, for example, may indicate Qi deficiency, whereas a red tongue with a yellow coating may indicate excess heat.

Listening and smelling entail focusing on the patient's speech, breath, and body odor. Changes in these variables can provide information about the underlying imbalances.

TCM practitioners frequently question emotional well-being and lifestyle, as these factors are critical to gaining a comprehensive knowledge of the patient's health.

Questioning allows you to learn more about the patient's symptoms, medical history, and lifestyle.

TCM practitioners inquire about the type, duration, and severity of symptoms, as well as any things that may aggravate or alleviate them.

Understanding the patient's emotional condition is critical, as emotions are thought to be a vital element in Qi balance.

Palpation entails feeling the pulse and analyzing certain bodily locations. The pulse not only measures the heartbeat but also indicates the quality and strength of Qi in various meridians. TCM practitioners are trained to detect small fluctuations in the pulse, which allows them to pinpoint organ imbalances.

Overall, TCM diagnosis is a thorough procedure that takes into account both the physical and emotional elements of the patient. TCM practitioners may customize treatment programs to address the fundamental causes of ailments and enhance general well-being by understanding the interaction of Qi and the balance of the body's systems.

Therapies Of Traditional Chinese Medicine

Traditional Chinese Medicine (TCM) is a collection of treatments focused on restoring balance and harmony to the body, mind, and spirit. These therapies, which have their roots in ancient Chinese philosophy, have evolved over thousands of years and remain essential to holistic healing. Acupuncture, herbal medicine, cupping treatment, moxibustion, and Tui Na massage are all important TCM therapies.

One of the most well-known TCM treatments is acupuncture, which involves inserting small needles into particular spots on the body. These points are placed along the meridians, and it is thought that stimulating these points regulates the flow of Qi, encouraging balance and healing. Acupuncture is widely used to treat a variety of ailments, including pain, tension, and emotional disorders.

Herbal medicine is another pillar of TCM, with a long history of employing plants, minerals, and animal products to treat. TCM practitioners recommend herbal formulae that are unique to the individual's imbalances and symptoms. Herbs are chosen not only for their therapeutic capabilities but also for their synergistic potential to address the underlying causes of sickness.

Cupping therapy includes applying suction cups to the skin to promote blood flow and Qi circulation. This method is frequently utilized for pain alleviation and muscle relaxation. Moxibustion, on the other hand, is the practice of burning mugwort on or near acupuncture sites to warm and energize the Qi, resolving cold or deficiency-related diseases.

Tui Na massage is a type of Chinese therapeutic massage in which various regions of the body are kneaded, rolled, and pressed. Its goal is to promote relaxation and relieve physical and emotional strain by stimulating the flow of Qi and blood.

These TCM therapies are frequently used in conjunction with a comprehensive treatment plan that is tailored to the individual's particular constitution and health needs. TCM's holistic nature acknowledges the interdependence of physical and mental well-being, and treatments are meant to address both components to restore balance and harmony.

Emotional Balance Acupuncture

For decades, acupuncture, a crucial component of Traditional Chinese Medicine (TCM), has been utilized to enhance emotional well-being and mental health. Emotions are directly tied to the flow of Qi, the vital energy that flows through the body's meridians, according to TCM principles. Imbalances in Qi can cause emotional disturbances, and acupuncture can help restore equilibrium and relieve emotional discomfort.

Acupuncture is a treatment that includes inserting tiny needles into particular acupuncture spots along the body's meridians. These points are picked based on the particular constitution of the individual and the precise emotional imbalances they are experiencing. Acupuncture is said to control the flow of Qi, correcting both excesses and deficiencies to bring the body and mind into balance.

Acupuncture is frequently used to treat emotional well-being issues such as stress, anxiety, depression, and sleeplessness.

The acupuncture sites used may target the liver, spleen, heart, and other organs related to emotional control in Traditional Chinese Medicine. Acupuncture attempts to treat emotional symptoms and improve general mental health by encouraging the smooth passage of Qi and balancing the energy of these organs.

According to research on the benefits of acupuncture on emotional well-being, it may impact neurotransmitters and hormones involved in mood regulation. Acupuncture may promote the release of endorphins, the body's natural painkillers, and modify sympathetic nervous system activity, facilitating relaxation and stress reduction.

Furthermore, acupuncture is frequently used as part of a multifaceted treatment plan that may include other TCM treatments, lifestyle changes, and dietary advice.

When developing a treatment approach, TCM practitioners evaluate the individual's total health and constitution, understanding the interconnection of physical and emotional well-being.

While acupuncture has demonstrated potential in achieving emotional balance, it is important to emphasize that individual reactions may differ. Some people may feel instant relief, while others may need many sessions to see meaningful results. Furthermore, when conducted by qualified practitioners, acupuncture is widely regarded as safe, making it a good alternative for people seeking a comprehensive approach to emotional well-being.

CHAPTER THREE

Emotional Well-Being Herbal Medicine

Herbal medicine is an important part of Traditional Chinese Medicine (TCM), which has been used for millennia to improve emotional well-being and manage mental health disorders. TCM considers the mind and body to be inextricably linked, and imbalances in the body's Qi can appear as emotional problems. Herbal therapy seeks to restore balance and harmony by combining unique medicinal characteristics of plants, minerals, and animal products.

TCM practitioners administer herbal formulae depending on the specific constitution, symptoms, and emotional imbalances of each individual. Herbs are chosen based on their energy qualities, flavors, and affinities to certain organs or meridians. These formulations are frequently designed to address the underlying causes of emotional disorders rather than simply soothing symptoms.

TCM medicines often used for emotional well-being include:

1. Ginseng (Ren Shen): Ginseng is known for its adaptogenic characteristics, which help the body adapt to stress and regulate the neurological system. It is frequently used to boost resilience and provide a sense of calm.

2. Rhodiola (Hong Jing Tian): Rhodiola is an adaptogen that is thought to help the body's reaction to stress and boost mental and physical performance. It may help alleviate anxiety and tiredness symptoms.

3. Jujube Seed (Suan Zao Ren): Jujube seed is commonly used to soothe the mind and induce relaxation. It is also used in recipes for insomnia, anxiety, and irritability.

4. Polygala Root (Yuan Zhi): Polygala root is traditionally used to quiet the soul and cleanse the mind and is used in formulae for ailments like as sleeplessness, anxiety, and forgetfulness.

5. Lily Bulb (Bai He): Used in formulae for diseases like as sleeplessness, palpitations, and anxiety, the lily bulb is known for its soothing effects.

TCM herbal formulae are frequently administered in combination to maximize therapeutic benefits and treat many elements of emotional well-being. Herbal medicine is a comprehensive approach that analyzes not just the symptoms but also the underlying imbalances in the body that may lead to emotional difficulties.

It's vital to remember that herbal therapy is highly customized in TCM, with formulae being altered based on the patient's reaction. TCM practitioners may also make food and lifestyle advice to help with general health.

While herbal medicine may be a helpful tool for improving emotional balance, it is critical to check with a skilled TCM practitioner before using it.

Emotional Harmony With Qi Gong And Tai Chi

Qi Gong and Tai Chi are ancient Chinese practices that combine physical movement, breath control, and mindfulness to enhance general health and emotional balance. These mind-body exercises, based on Traditional Chinese Medicine (TCM) principles, are intended to develop and balance the flow of Qi, the essential life energy said to underpin health and vigor.

Qi Gong: Qi Gong, which translates as "energy cultivation," refers to a variety of exercises and meditation practices. The major emphasis is on nurturing and balancing Qi to improve physical, mental, and emotional well-being. Gentle motions, breathwork, visualization, and meditation are all possible Qi Gong activities.

Qi Gong strives to regulate the flow of Qi through the body's meridians in the context of emotional well-being, treating imbalances that may contribute to emotional suffering.

Regular practice is thought to aid in the release of stagnated energy, the reduction of tension, and the enhancement of the body's inherent healing capacities.

Qi Gong exercises for emotional balance may include techniques that target the heart and liver meridians, which are related to emotional control in Traditional Chinese Medicine. Breathwork and meditation practices are frequently used to help relax the mind and achieve inner peace.

Tai Chi: Also known as "meditation in motion," Tai Chi is a martial art that mixes slow, flowing motions with deep diaphragmatic breathing and concentrated attention. Tai Chi, like Qi Gong, is based on TCM principles and strives to balance and harmonize the body's Qi.

Tai Chi's slow and methodical motions are intended to induce relaxation, improve balance, and increase Qi flow. Regular Tai Chi practice has been linked to a variety of health advantages, including stress reduction, increased mood, and general well-being.

Tai Chi promotes the connection of mind and body in terms of emotional harmony, producing a sense of mindfulness and presence. The concentration on the present moment, as well as the coordination of movement and breath, can have a soothing impact on the neurological system, aiding in the relief of anxiety and stress symptoms.

People of all ages and fitness levels can participate in Qi Gong and Tai Chi. They may be tailored to individual requirements and used in a variety of contexts, making them useful instruments for enhancing emotional well-being. While these techniques can be useful on their own, they can also be used in conjunction with other Traditional Chinese Medicine therapies to provide a more comprehensive approach to health.

Finally, by combining movement, breath, and awareness, Qi Gong and Tai Chi provide unique routes to emotional peace. These practices, which have their roots in Traditional Chinese Medicine, provide people with the skills they need to create balance and enhance general well-being in the interrelated worlds of body, mind, and spirit.

Traditional Chinese Medicine Diet & Nutrition

Traditional Chinese Medicine (TCM) sees the human body as a holistic system in which the balance of energy, or Qi, is critical to health. Diet and nutrition are important components of TCM since they contribute considerably to Qi balance and overall well-being. dietary is considered a type of medicine in TCM, and the dietary choices we make may have a significant influence on our physical, mental, and emotional health.

TCM principles state that various meals have varied energetic characteristics that can either replenish or deplete the body's vital energy. TCM philosophy's underlying principle of Yin and Yang extends to food categorization. Yin meals are chilly, moist, and nourishing, whereas Yang foods are heated, dry, and energizing. A harmonic balance of Yin and Yang is vital for good health.

TCM suggests a diet that is compatible with the individual's constitution and present health situation to achieve emotional equilibrium. Someone who has too much heat in their body, for example, may benefit from cooling foods like cucumbers, melons, and leafy greens to help balance the system. Individuals with a Qi shortage, on the other hand, may be encouraged to take warming foods such as ginger, garlic, and hearty soups.

TCM incorporates the Five Elements (Wood, Fire, Earth, Metal, Water) in dietary recommendations in addition to the energy characteristics of food. Each element connects to different organs and emotions, and an imbalance in any element might have an impact on one's emotional well-being. A person with a Wood element imbalance, for example, may feel irritable or angry, and altering their diet to support the liver and gallbladder might help restore balance.

Furthermore, TCM stresses mindful eating, urging people to be present and grateful for their food. Chewing, enjoying, and digesting food is thought to be essential to the body's capacity to absorb nutrients and maintain equilibrium. TCM also encourages eating frequent, balanced meals and avoids eating cold or raw foods in excess, since they might weaken the digestive system and contribute to imbalances.

CHAPTER FOUR

Traditional Chinese Medicine's Mind-Body Connection

Recognizing the complicated connections between mental and physical health is a major part of Traditional Chinese Medicine. Emotions, according to TCM, are both a reflection of and an impact on the status of the body's Qi. The smooth movement of Qi requires emotional equilibrium, and any interruption in this flow can lead to bodily and mental discord.

Emotions are strongly associated with certain organs in TCM, and an imbalance in one might impact the other. Excessive anger, for example, is linked to the liver, pleasure to the heart, concern to the spleen, mourning to the lungs, and fear to the kidneys. Chronic or severe emotional moods might interfere with the passage of Qi in various organs, potentially resulting in physical diseases.

TCM incorporates mind-body activities including acupuncture, tai chi, and qigong, which are said to assist in regulating the flow of Qi and restore equilibrium.

Acupuncture, which involves inserting small needles into precise places on the body, is supposed to release trapped energy while also alleviating mental and physical ailments. Tai chi and qigong, on the other hand, are gentle workouts that encourage Qi flow via focused movements and deep breathing.

TCM also recognizes the influence of lifestyle variables on the mind-body link. Maintaining emotional equilibrium is said to require enough relaxation, stress management, and the cultivation of pleasant emotions.

Meditation and herbal therapies are also used to help with mental well-being. Adaptogenic herbs, such as ginseng and rhodiola, are thought to help the body adapt to stress and enhance general resilience.

Traditional Chinese Medicine's Emotional Imbalances

Emotions are regarded as a natural and vital component of life in Traditional Chinese Medicine, and their influence on health is well recognized. Emotional discord is considered an interruption in the flow of Qi, resulting in disharmony within the body. TCM acknowledges a clear link between distinct emotions and their effects on various organs, providing a unique viewpoint on emotional well-being.

Anger, which is related to the liver, is viewed as an emotion that, when excessive or protracted, can lead to Qi stagnation in the liver. This might appear as irritation, headaches, or stomach problems. Joy, which is related to the heart, is regarded as helpful in moderation, but excessive joy can upset the equilibrium of the heart, perhaps leading to sleeplessness or restlessness. Worry and overthinking, which are related to the spleen, can weaken the digestive system and lead to weariness and digestive problems. Grief that affects the lungs might cause respiratory issues or a compromised immune system. Fear, which is linked to the kidneys, can affect the adrenal glands and lead to disorders such as sleeplessness and exhaustion.

TCM practitioners evaluate emotional imbalances by taking into account the exact emotions a person feels, their severity, and the organs involved. This integrative approach enables a customized treatment plan that addresses both the emotional and physical components of well-being. Herbal medicines, acupuncture, dietary changes, and lifestyle suggestions are prominent methods for restoring balance.

TCM also emphasizes the significance of developing emotional intelligence and resilience. To increase emotional awareness and balance, mindful activities such as meditation, breathwork, and self-reflection are advised. TCM also acknowledges the interdependence of emotions, stressing that treating one emotional imbalance can have a good impact on others.

Approaches To Emotional Disorders In Traditional Chinese Medicine

Traditional Chinese Medicine holistically treats emotional illnesses, acknowledging the interdependence of the mind, body, and spirit. TCM practitioners seek to restore balance by addressing the underlying cause of emotional imbalances rather than simply treating symptoms. Here are some important TCM techniques for emotional disorders:

1. Acupuncture is an ancient therapy in which fine needles are inserted into precise places on the body to promote the flow of Qi. Acupuncture is said to unblock energy and restore balance, treating both physical and emotional ailments.

2. TCM employs a diverse spectrum of herbs to promote emotional well-being. Adaptogenic herbs such as ginseng, ashwagandha, and Rhodiola are

frequently given to assist the body in adapting to stress and promoting general resilience.

3. TCM emphasizes the importance of nutrition in maintaining emotional equilibrium. To improve emotional wellness, dietary changes such as adopting certain foods to nourish weak organs or avoiding items that lead to excess are suggested.

4. Mind-Body Practices: Tai chi and qigong, both of which include gentle movements and deep breathing, are used to regulate Qi flow and create emotional equilibrium. Meditation and mindfulness are also important tools for developing emotional awareness.

5. Lifestyle Advice: TCM practitioners offer advice on lifestyle variables that impact emotional well-being. To maintain total balance, adequate rest, stress management, and the cultivation of pleasant emotions are stressed.

6. Emotional Release Techniques: TCM understands the significance of expressing and processing emotions. Breathing exercises, writing, and therapy

can all be used to help release pent-up emotions and promote emotional recovery.

7. TCM practitioners frequently utilize tongue and pulse diagnostics to examine the level of Qi and discover particular abnormalities. This diagnostic technique aids in tailoring treatment approaches to each individual's specific needs.

8. Seasonal Changes: TCM acknowledges the impact of seasonal changes on the body and emotions. Treatment strategies may be modified, including dietary suggestions and herbal prescriptions, to correspond with seasonal effects and preserve balance.

To summarize, Traditional Chinese Medicine offers a complete and holistic approach to emotional balance, addressing the deep relationships between the mind, body, and emotions. TCM offers tailored ways to restore equilibrium and promote long-term emotional health by taking the individual's constitution, emotional patterns, and general well-being into account. TCM strives to not only treat symptoms but also address the core causes of emotional imbalances via the integration of acupuncture, herbal medicine, food therapy, and mind-body activities, creating a profound feeling of well-being.

<u>CHAPTER FIVE</u>

Case Studies In Traditional Chinese Medicine On Emotional Balance

In Traditional Chinese Medicine (TCM), emotional equilibrium is a critical component of total well-being. TCM considers emotions to be related to the organs and energy systems of the body and believes that imbalances can appear as physical diseases. Several case studies demonstrate TCM's effectiveness in healing emotional disorders.

A patient with persistent stress and anxiety endured acupuncture treatments that targeted particular meridian points connected with the liver and heart. TCM associates these organs with emotional control.

After a few sessions, the patient reported considerable decreases in anxiety and increased sleep, demonstrating TCM's comprehensive approach to emotional well-being.

Another example involved melancholy and exhaustion. TCM practitioners supplied a personalized herbal mix and suggested dietary changes by TCM principles. The patient's attitude and energy levels gradually improved over several weeks. TCM's holistic approach to emotional balance was proven through the integration of acupuncture, herbal medicines, and lifestyle changes.

Bringing Traditional Chinese Medicine And Western Medicine Together

The combination of Traditional Chinese Medicine and Western medicine is a viable paradigm for total healthcare. Recognizing both systems' capabilities, a synergistic approach has the potential to improve patient outcomes.

A combination of acupuncture and Western pain management treatments has shown outstanding results in the treatment of chronic pain. According to TCM principles, acupuncture relieves pain by improving the passage of Qi. Patients frequently receive more thorough relief when combined with Western pain medicines and physical therapy.

Collaborative methods for emotional problems have evolved. TCM therapies such as acupuncture and herbal medicines can supplement psychiatric care, medication, and psychotherapy. This integrated approach recognizes the complex link between the mind and body, aiming for a more comprehensive therapeutic method.

Clinical trials have looked into the advantages of combining TCM and Western therapies. Acupuncture research and the use of herbal medicines in cancer therapy emphasize the possibility of merging these two systems to enhance patient outcomes.

Traditional Chinese Medicine Research And Evidence

TCM's incorporation with Western medicine has resulted in increasing examination of TCM procedures via rigorous research approaches. While obstacles remain, new research has offered important insights into the processes and efficacy of TCM therapies.

Acupuncture, a defining feature of TCM, has been a focus of study. Acupuncture has been shown in research to modify brain activity, impacting pain perception and emotional control. RCTs assessing acupuncture for illnesses such as chronic pain and insomnia have yielded positive findings, adding to the expanding body of data supporting its usefulness.

TCM herbal medicine has also been scrutinized. Meta-analyses of RCTs investigating the benefits of individual herbal formulations on illnesses such as irritable bowel syndrome and eczema have yielded good results.

TCM's emphasis on tailored therapies challenges standardization while emphasizing the need for personalized approaches in research.

However, difficulties remain in developing a coherent research framework for TCM. Obstacles include placebo effects, variation in herbal formulations, and the requirement for culturally acceptable outcome metrics. Collaboration between

TCM practitioners and Western scholars is critical for resolving these issues and expanding the evidence basis for TCM.

Traditional Chinese Medicine's Cultural Perspectives On Emotional Health

Understanding emotional health in the context of TCM necessitates diving into cultural ideas that have affected TCM for generations. TCM considers emotions to be vital components of a person's entire health, taking into account the connection between emotional well-being, physical health, and the surrounding environment.

Emotions are related to certain organs and energy pathways in TCM. Anger, for example, is associated with the liver, pleasure with the heart, concern with the spleen, sadness with the lungs, and fear with the kidneys. Imbalances in these emotions can impair Qi flow and cause sickness. This integrated perspective represents a holistic knowledge of the person in the context of nature.

TCM's approach to emotional wellness is also influenced by cultural components such as the notion of Yin and Yang. TCM strives to preserve equilibrium by balancing the opposing forces of Yin (passive, receptive) and Yang (active, dynamic). Emotional disturbances are frequently viewed as disruptions in this delicate balance, and TCM remedies try to restore balance.

Emotional Balance And Future Trends In Traditional Chinese Medicine

Traditional Chinese Medicine's function in emotional balance has great prospects in the future. TCM is anticipated to play a more important role in conventional healthcare as interest in holistic and integrative medicine rises.

Technological advancements may aid in the modernization of TCM methods. TCM practitioners might use wearable gadgets and biofeedback tools to monitor patients' Qi flow and energy balance, giving vital data for tailored treatment strategies. Integrating TCM concepts into digital health platforms may improve accessibility and enable remote consultations.

Collaborative research endeavors linking TCM and Western medicine are anticipated to grow in the future. The evidence foundation will be strengthened by establishing standardized research methodologies, investigating biomarkers for TCM diagnosis, and performing large-scale clinical trials. This partnership might result in the creation of integrated treatment recommendations, promoting a more unified and patient-centered approach to healthcare.

TCM's future will also be shaped by educational programs. Integrating TCM ideas into medical school curricula and encouraging multidisciplinary training for healthcare workers can help healthcare professionals get a more thorough grasp of holistic treatment. This will help to create a healthcare system in which TCM and Western medicine live together, providing patients with a varied variety of treatment alternatives.

Finally, the approach to emotional balance taken by Traditional Chinese Medicine, as supported by case studies, integration with Western medicine, growing research, cultural perspectives, and future tendencies, provides a dynamic picture of a system profoundly anchored in holistic well-being. TCM's rich past continues to give vital insights into the delicate link between emotions, the body, and the environment as the lines between traditional and contemporary medicine blur. Accepting this integration can pave the way for a more holistic and patient-centered approach to healthcare in the coming years.

Conclusion

Finally, Traditional Chinese Medicine (TCM) has long acknowledged the complex relationship between emotional well-being and physical health. TCM regards emotional disturbances as possible contributors to sickness since it is based on the notion of harmonizing the body's essential energy, or qi. TCM tries to restore physical harmony by treating mental imbalances using treatments like acupuncture, herbal medicine, and Qigong.

TCM provides a comprehensive approach to emotional equilibrium by emphasizing the interdependence of mind and body. The meridian system, via which energy flows throughout the body, is thought to impact both physical and emotional states. Acupuncture, for example, regulates energy flow and relieves emotional discomfort by targeting particular sites along these meridians.

Herbal treatments are also frequently adapted to individual constitutions, addressing not just physical ailments but also emotional proclivities. TCM understands the influence of emotions on organ function and general health, such as stress, rage, and sadness. TCM attempts to achieve balance by improving emotional resilience and avoiding disease through a tailored and complete approach.

TCM's comprehensive approach to emotional balance is a beneficial supplement to conventional treatments in an era when mental health is increasingly acknowledged as a vital component of total well-being. TCM stands out as a time-tested method that bridges the gap between emotional and physical balance as individuals seek holistic ways for health and recovery.